Also By Gerard Malanga

3 Poems For Benedetta Barzini (1967)
Prelude To International Velvet Debutante (1967)
Screen Tests / A Diary, in collaboration with Andy Warhol (1967)
The Last Benedetta Poems (1969)
cristinas world (1970)
Gerard Malanga Selbsportrat eines Dichters (1970)
10 Poems For 10 Poets (1970)
the blue book (1970)
beatle calendar (1970)
chic death (1971)
poetry on film (1972)
Wheels of Light (1972)
The Poetry of Night, Dawn and Dream / Nine Poems for César Vallejo (1972)
A Portfolio of Four Duographs, in collaboration with A. T. Mann (1973)
Licht / Light (1973, bilingual)
7 Poems For Pilar Crespi (1973)
Incarnations: Poems 1965-1971 (1974)
Rosebud (1975)
Leaping Over Gravestones (1976)
Bringing Up Baby (1977)
Ten Years After: The Selected Benedetta Poems (1977)
100 years have passed (1978)
This Will Kill That (1983)

SELECTED COMPILATIONS

Transatlantic Review #52 – An Anthology of New American Poetry (1975)
Little Caesar #9 / "Unprecedented Information" (1979)
Angus MacLise Checklist 1959-1979 (1981)

GERARD MALANGA

THIS WILL KILL THAT

BLACK SPARROW PRESS
SANTA BARBARA   1983

6/1983
Am Lit/Cont

ACKNOWLEDGEMENT

Grateful acknowledgement is made to the following publications in which some of these poems first appeared (some in somewhat different form): *Burnt Sienna #1, Glassworks, Himma, Hot Water Review, Illuminati, Little Caesar,* and *Painted Bride Quarterly.*

Acknowledgement is also made to Black Sparrow Press for its use of "Things to Know" and "Devotion" in its serial pamphlet publication *Sparrow* (#48) Copyright © 1976 by Gerard Malanga, and for "*Briefe an* Maxwell Perkins" and "All Hallows' Eve" in *Sparrow* (#66) Copyright © 1978 by Gerard Malanga; to New Directions Publishing Corporation for its first publication use of "Ananké," "This Will Kill That" and "Little Italy" in its annual anthology *New Directions #36* (1978) edited by J. Laughlin (with Peter Glassgold & Frederick R. Martin).

Part II of this book includes several of the poems that originally appeared in the book publication *Bringing Up Baby* by Gerard Malanga, privately printed in a signed and numbered edition of 22 copies Copyright © 1977 by Gerard Malanga.

Poem quoted on p. 53 in "Q: What are you feeling? A: Guilty." is entitled "A Poem for Gerard Malanga" by Lew Welch (1926-1971?) from *Ring of Bone, Collected Poems 1950-1971,* Grey Fox Press. Copyright © 1973 by Don Allen, Literary Executor of the Estate of Lew Welch.

Cover: "Perseus Slays Medusa" (relief) by Edmond Romulius Amateis (1897-   ).

Half-title photographs for Parts I, II, and III by Gerard Malanga.

Half-title photograph for Part IV: *Notre Dame de Paris* by Patras, ca. 1920s. Collection: Malanga.

Thanks to Sonia Raiziss Giop for time spent on refining the essay.

LIBRARY OF CONGRESS CATALOGING IN PUBLICATION DATA

Malanga, Gerard.
    This will kill that.

    I. Title.
PS3563.A42I5   1983   811'.54   83-8731
ISBN 0-87685-496-X (signed ed.)
ISBN 0-87685-495-1 (pbk.)

To my friend
David Rattray
in admiration and affection

CONTENTS

I
THE AGE OF PERICLES

II
BRINGING UP BABY

III
dal vero

IV
THIS WILL KILL THAT
an experiment in autobiography

THIS WILL KILL THAT

I do not intend to tell the particulars of the women I have been to bed with, or anything about them. Don't look for it. . . . I am extremely sexual in my desires: I carry them everywhere and at all times. I think that from that arises the drive which empowers us all. Given that drive, a man does with it what his mind directs. In the manner in which he directs that power lies his secret.

—William Carlos Williams
Foreword, *The Autobiography*

I

THE AGE OF PERICLES

I found myself suddenly and hopelessly entangled with someone I had admired some years before but never quite imagined in the context of a lover. Chance brought us together for a few short months. I think that neither of us had foreseen this sudden coup de foudre. *We both caught fire as if somewhere an invisible burning glass had been playing on us without our being aware. It is curious that an experience so wounding can also be recognised as good, as positively nourishing.*

—Lawrence Durrell, *Clea*

Tie Dye

clouds are being swept across the sky
the sun sets

elsewhere
leaving its light
as your eyes

11:iii: 1971, nyc

Things to Know

The first English Grammar was not written
until twenty years after
Shakespeare was dead.

*

A comma (,) was a slight pause
and a period (.) was a full stop.

Spelling was a question of style,
and not law and order.

*

You speak with your eyes.

Devotion

Words
simply given
or else eyes—

endlessly
poised

and
turning
the page

recognize
the force of
the full moon

as if an image
in my life
returned

—a birch woods,

knowing
ways
to such places
all distances
embrace more

as far as the
earth in any
direction, goes

and, likewise,
makes therefore
a very different
way of seeing—

the simple
truth of
the intention,

or what's felt
as a presence,

an aura of sorts,
that cannot
be measured.

What inspires you,
gives you
pleasure, then   as now
to listen to,
among other things,
words,
so that the sense I have
of you is all I have

Your silence, at moments,
would be the answer, the heart
of the matter, the
rain which follows
out the window. Tomorrow
reoccurs, so
that there's no
conclusion of
events past,
but the one
consistent blur

Where are you now
for that matter?

It is not in the important things
that I see differently,
but in the unimportant things

the co
inci
dence of
meeting

that is, what does one do
against a feeling like
giving
as opposed to

discovering
life or death,
as human, also?

Memories
have a place
in the mind—in the heart, too—

renders service of
an essential and intimate kind.

The body sleeps,
but the mind remains constant.

Does the mind dream?

What dreams?

What if all breathing
stopped?

K a r*

To suggest resounding praise
I have none.

I walk out into a birchwoods
of a photo
            framed
on a desk.
And sunlight

covers this desk
in the day when you are away.

The silence surrounds.

The silence
surrounds

Only that. Only that.

---

* The root: "to praise loudly, extol"; *Kāru*—in Greek (Doric); in Russian *krasa*, beauty, "a thing to be extolled"—*American Heritage Dictionary*

Private Moments Only

Sometimes, the mind cannot hang
to feelings as to words.

Sometimes, words are not conclusive
rendering or focus to remote yearnings,
or to the immediate present
of what's evident as feeling.

Nothing grand . . .
such is the fact of us,
insofar as one
can speak of the other.

I remember
you saying, "I am so happy"
brushing beside me
in the kitchen,

or of the photo taken by Barbara—

you guiding your parents,
holding onto your father
by the elbow,
a simplicity and grace of
black dress about you . . .

so very much this same quiet now
tangent to another quiet:

your mouth,
opening,
rot speaking,
touches.

Or else a breeze comes through the window
and I get up to go to the window.
Night inside the room
and further out airplane landing-lights.
The moon's light on your face.

And whatever is said
not said, makes a form,
a legacy.

These hands,
this face.

The sound of pen on paper.

A moment ago it was night.
Now daylight.

The hands on the bedsheet find quiet.

The city is waking.

What way now will be its gift to me
will be its gift to you

The Future Now

I have called my whole life
into question
having no need for answers
in a rational world
that provides only rational answers.

I take my chances
as I know of
no other way, except that
it occurs, a private moment
on which I stake myself:

words of such reassurance
you uttered
I felt somehow blessed
and privileged, too.

Why do you fear me
now? Why?

Twenty, thirty years go by.
Suddenly you wake up, realize
time does not stand still.
But you will
go about the day's business
in the rational world
that provides only rational answers
to help you
forget and with reason

the giving and taking
the singular trust
the wish for three more wishes
wishing to come true

as it must
surely

what was sacrificed because you
let down your defenses
and didn't mean to

or else
something like courage

and it was simple enough:

your hand on my back
as if to protect me;
something heroic like that
as I remember correctly
a night on Hudson Street
hailing a taxi

the casualness of the encounter
years ago . . .

not now. Things continue
It is that we grow
older in a world of no
one else.

Don't pretend. Don't just die.

Don't ask forgiveness
whatever love was
once,
finally

the photographs fade—
all senses including the mind
as dreams are, when the day wakes
now tangent to another time.

Then it was morning

a cup of coffee

a cigarette out of "need"

You stare out through the window
at an emptiness of wind and rain.

A feeling like pain
enters the throat

Auto-portrait at 1/5th

I'm not sure
anymore.

The perpetual
reservation of
judgment

and the perpetual
choosing

Belchertown.
Oneonta.
Wainscott.
NY.

Series of choices
Sequence, of sorts.

Place-names
not quite the same.

The choices
dissolve, one
at a time

or is it
one day follows
another

and then
the weeks, several,
and for each, several
poems

Books

and people.

People and trees.

And photographs, too.

The music is disco
through the walls.

There's no
going back
to what I know.

                 *

Karen lives
upstairs

is what I'm reminded
when I step into 1/5th.

HEY, GIRL!

Karen engaged

to be married

is what I'm told
by Dorothy Dean.

Water seeks its own level,
or so it seems.

The body dies
in its dreams.

                 *

What's beneath
that counts
doesn't seem to count
with some of
the people
I care
for

all of the time.

Break
what I can
reach

is not
the answer.

Solutions
are not
the answer

but
a level
of clarity

agreement
of feeling

One pays for
what one can't afford

through the nose

is not always the case,
or it is, so to speak.

One is content

or not content,
I suppose.

What one is satisfied
with

is not
what
one wishes

One wishes more

of what
one already has

*

Each morning
the sky
bright blue
or slate gray

the sun on
the high-rise
across the street

Will a poem
come
of it

I can see it all
I can see it all
I can see it all
I can see it all

A Last Poem

Times
when I think of you
but don't want to

and you keep cropping up
in odd ways
on cold days

like walking
University Place,
for instance

I stop for
the light
at E. 8th

turns green

or I stop
anyway

the sun
trying
to rise
in the windows

the blinds
half-drawn

in one,
sometimes two

a clue
to your
absence

or presence

or the rooms
fully-lit

and suddenly
you appear
in the bathroom

You're already there

or it's simply
weeks

or years
later

Where was it
we had been

central
to my thoughts
of you

a room to
walk around in

to stand in
to talk in—

again
and
again

some sense
of limit

         begins
to move with
or from

Some other person
or place

inseparable
from the past

but continuous

You begin to live only when you have abandoned, rejected all solutions.

—Lawrence Durrell

It is an ashtray of dead cigarettes
singing

and beside it
a photo of someone

in the night waking
cars rumbling

the sound of metal
awnings being rolled down

or is it the wind

it is distraction

it is a cover-up

it is a rumor

it is trying to forget
what I mustn't forget

it is mind
and memory
speaking

it works
out of a self
imposed silence

it moves in three directions
simultaneously

it is the overthrow of time
it is powerless

it is unresolved—has no solutions

it could have been
many other things

night of rain
a weekend

the turning of leaves

events realized

unrealized

it is lacking

nothing to revise;
therefore, it changes
nothing

it tries
to imagine itself
not written yet

it has nothing to do with love
is a lie

it declares nothing,
even after the lie

it is waking
and dreaming

it is needed

it is abandoned

for Phil Bleeth

II

BRINGING UP BABY

The assumption that the artist seeks only success and fame originates with the unproductive type [the neurotic] who may not only be eager for it himself, but also be actuated by the belief that the artist wants to become famous, whereas really he himself wants to make him famous so as to participate in his immortality.

—Otto Rank, *Art & Artist*

Ich bin schuldig

Wainscott

You hold your dress
and walk
into
the spray.

A lovely presence.

A White Dress

Something in me remembers
and will not forget
the first time

A specific circumstance.

Yet I could feel a presence,
sense a warmth.

But something in you
remembers—

leads me to believe
there was an intelligence
working

And this I felt attractive

what attracted me
to you.

Then why
this anger

towards you
and towards myself?

Misgiving

How are you

What have you to show
for your troubles

A black eye—

aching for a fucking
bruise, like they say

Don't hate me for the poems I write,
if what I write
is what you hate

in yourself.

What's at stake

Patience. Solitude.

A clarity of mind.

A walk in the woods.

A confidence.

A Love Poem, of sorts

I suspect even as a child you were a late sleeper
making a fool of yourself finally
and then taking it out on everyone else—
pitting fear against fear,
which is only human nature, I suppose—
and then to apologize
as if that were enough to not feel guilt
for it to happen again
in betraying someone's feelings
and your own.

I did
think I did
not mishear
you when you said "idear"
[*sic*] for idea.

I'm not one to pride myself on correct pronunciation.
We have our charm, you know.

We're not that far from being unafraid.

You Speak

Here is the
word, *there*
is its means
to get somewhere.

Words open, somehow
begin. Then let them.

For the time being,
let me speak.
Let me
find a way
out of words.

You speak.

Sentiment/ality

What way
now might there be
a place
of something—

after years?

Q: *What are you feeling?*
A: *Guilty.*

A photo
of someone

taking off clothes
in the one
room's light

a photo of someone

in sudden sun
light, even

from
years ago

A feeling comes
and goes

a see-thru curtain
in and out the window

is all rhythm

to know
where
one is—

Massachusetts

New York

Rte 22

A sequence, of sorts.

Conversations with Jim.
The intervals

The continual
sense of moving
through distance and time

a series of
road-signs

long
stretches of
fence-post

The moon waning
as if all life were
waning

stars and small planets,
fading.

*

In bed
just waking
up

See the trees,
all around
sleeping

the sky flat out

Or the wind
in its silence—

birches folded
into patterns
of sound

birds long since
gone, through.

Nests frozen over.

The leaves.
The grass.

A smoke haze,
instead

burning.

Partial clearings

Clouds
broken
at last
open

Frost and sun
later.

Not now.
Not warm enough

Not even
warm enough
to take a
quick run.

The mind
takes
its time

to forget

to remember

moves backwards

Or moves
forward:

the inside
of a car
traveling north.

Trees flashing by.
The night outside.

Sun shining
as moonlight.

I feel right.
I want to.

You look
around you

insisting
everyone knows
me!

A petulance

a quiet
desperation

a foolishness,
of sorts.

All that to
what purpose?

Nobody knows
us

I tell you

not giving a good goddamn
who does!

Then why ask?

Rather, you feel
the mark of one who's met people
with no time lost

Not a presumption—

but the fact of

a
particular
circumstance.

*

I'm a different person
to many people.

Too many people.

Who is this person
Who is this person
Who is that person

Who is *you?*

Am I happy

Are you needed

What difference
does it make?

I sleep I dream I wake
I die also

Fears included.

*

Affection
invents
intelligence

the associations
one makes
in the mind—

some sense of
depth in thought

absorbed
in some thing

to be alone,
so to speak—

peace of
mind,

or

night of
another

day in or out

the endless, frightening
people
one tries
to avoid

The crush
like they say

space-wise.

Where can you hide,

why do you want to?

What's it like to
feel ambition?

What scares
you?

Am I to wear
dark glasses

grow fingernails
two inches long

skin to the bone

hair down past
my shoulders

What's it prove?

I grow bored
having to
explain myself

I want nothing of
reference points
but what makes
you barren
of familial facts

and to show you
that view
from the window
of horses
hardly ridden
for months—

a walk in the woods

the sun fading
at 4 p.m.
behind Warner Mountain.

A silence
surrounds.

*

What is it
you want
to know?

Be specific!

See it out

or go utterly away
from all of it,

but don't talk
about it

events
meant
not only
for
the observer.

No one there.
No one.

What transforms?

You or me.

But the world
comes into focus,
also.

Not just hostile.
Not beyond us.

Life *is* lived.

Then, live it!

                    *

"More
people know
you than
you know."

A poet wrote
that,
thinking of me.

It was another life

The price of fame:

the aura
surrounding a name,
I suppose.

A myth in his own mind.
He's entitled to that.

He died before
I knew of the poem—

before I could ask.

*

Outside, a windy rain,
as I sit now
writing this

Six windows
One door

but who
enters

as if being
alone
would provide answers
patiently waited for

A dirt
road some day
will not be this
one

roughed out

but grown
over

I walk on it.
I look down on it.

Perhaps an emptiness
will come from it, perhaps
the sound of a lost animal
only

*

Is being
adored

or hated

a crime?

The past

the present

commingles

Who remembers?

One remembers

the people
the places

A room
providing warmth

the sounds of
feelings

opening
and closing

windows
and
doors

and closet doors,
too. Sometimes.

Hands
holding

a quiet

the moments
of one's life

my own life

the choices

made or not
made

or the voices

sometimes laughing
sometimes not

Places one means to
return to

don't change

now
and
then

or if they
do—

but as time returning

as measure

but also the pleasure
involved

the women one grew
up with

dead or gone

or of what couldn't be
then

but someone else
coming

someone guilty
someone insane

Beauty is not just skin
deep!

hands
hair
eyes

a lovely presence

                *

We share in these thoughts
that do not share

Yet I don't believe it

I'm not one to care
for figures of speech
or their function

just
words

just
people

12-26:xii:76   Sheffield, MA

Coda: "Bringing Up Baby"

Why must you
always make a point
of mistrust
in people,

insisted upon
so often?

Is it
the trust
someone had for you,

even the fulfillment,
what it must have been—

what must
it feel *to be liked*,
specifically

what reveals
to you,

that it be
disdainful

Must it be
every time

that whatever
constitutes space
and the people in it

is the unwillingness
to participate

to reject
outright

but in the mind
only

Or—whatever occasion
presents itself

where, one thought,
tenderness
was simply
a mind
feeling—

Always
the finally foolish
assumption
of what it will
be like and who will
be there

as being something there
that you are not:

A convenience
to allegations,

to point the finger

so to speak

to say someone
is patronizing—

What gives you
the right

What is
that is
finally so vicious
by its very nature
to be kind

the voice
vague

unsure
of itself

half-terrified.

Wanting reassurance—
not really wanting it.

Make up your mind.

Then what is
intelligence
for

if not capable
of continuance
and balance

moving, one
could say,
on the bare
ground

so that
in saying something,
something else unfolds

the sense of
continual

surprise

the sense of
distance
covered

or the space
one lies on
sleeping

I will walk in the woods.
I will not be a romantic.
I am not blind to beauty.

Fill it with yourself.

Tracking

I am alone.

A simplicity of
white walls
a table, some chairs
a few books, etc.

I begin to speak
with two voices.

One speaks to me,
the other
answers.

Sometimes
I think in
still another voice

not a mind
speaking but
sitting here

a mind
feeling

listening
to
itself

discovering
its response
as silence

the sense of myself,
now separate,

now self
containd

It is simply
voice

so called
in words

lacking
a face
or name

we give
it ours.

Violence is the expression of impotence.

—Hannah Arendt

Violence

Violence
is a specific
form of guilt

as
when someone
does you harm
ill-will

out of a
kindness
received

the choice
simply
a voice
in words

what's said
on the phone

an ineptness
to speak
convincingly

to
speak
convincingly

I cannot feel
wrong, about it—

refuse to
be made to

but as *to*
please by one
who feels
guilty
having felt
such pleasure
briefly

I want to
hear
laughter

Instead
this silence

in several
instances
this turning
away of
the head

this lack of
recognizable
attention

to the person speaking

Feelings of anger,
jealousy, meanness

for certain social
occasions

known to
no one
but yourself

the sudden
sense of
exposure

this lack of
trust

or the fear
of the way
you appear

in the
eyes of
others

the loss
of identity.

One is never
done with it
if
stuck in
that attitude.

For instance,
Eating is a specific
form of punishment

Song of Whales

Opposition creates time:

1907. 1917. 1968.

1977 and so on.

All memories are in the present.

Birds sing but we have invented a terrible silence.

The difference is inside the mind.

We cannot forgive ourselves. Therefore, there's violence.

I have only one debt that matters—

a clarity of mind

an agreement of feeling

the discovery of a lovely dignity

the care and reverence for written words as such.

It is a world of emptiness.

It is 1 p.m.

It is lack of trust.

You see sunlight coming in thru a window or you don't.

I am incapable of lies in this matter.

Ways and Means

risk
exist

spirit
committed.

Love Poem (tentative title)

We are simply
rumors of

what could
have been—

a walk by the seashore
at sunset

a
silence
to
fill

At daybreak there are only victims.

Lecture on Creeley

Running into
someone
one tries
not to avoid:

It's too easy—

matter of
timing, fact
of fate

West Broadway,
Prince,
to be exact.

Morning. Mid-day.

Snow on ground

Now sunlight.

Sky turning grey.

First time
seeing you
all bundled up

blue parka

white ice-skates

Memory becomes separation
until both fade
objectively,
as in

Days

weeks
months

sometimes years

a *continuance*

a flashback
in this instance

as the mind sees
it

voice grows
louder

more anxious

caught

wants to be free

wants

to be innocent

blameless

Stasis is
not the
answer if

making
decisions is

what you
enjoy

What is

a great
joy
to you
then

if what
effects
change

annoys
you

You walk off
call out *mean*
from far off

out of
reach—

It was done.

Something felt . . .

said
in childhood
perhaps

a door
shut
many years

this fear
of emptiness
for something
you've not become

nothing
has happened
at all

nothing gets done,
nothing really

gets even started

a goal
not reached

the risk
involved

the voice
not sweet

the voice
not sweet

never
mattered much

or if it did
there were
other attributes

There is grace
there is dignity

There is this walk
as I remember correctly

a potato field—

Wainscott

a hurricane
wipe-out

a series of
sand dunes

an open silence

the sun
behind us
fades

day comes
to an end

walking
back to
the house

build
fire

keep
warm.

Things
we did
not
talk about.

No need to.

Instead
a silence
to fill

with silence

What has
neurosis
replaced

if what is
feared is
affection

makes
clear
the mistrust

violence
bred of guilt
and from guilt
something to
believe

vanity

some thing
at least

Elsewise
a presence

a mind
speaking
there

One wants
to hurt
and not
get hurt

never
understood
that pleasure

Stick it
up your
ass

like they say

Simply say
what you feel

what you see—

if need be,
about yourself
even

in that mirror
even

up close

A reflection of feeling
is all it is

Don't mistake me
for someone else

Don't
mistake me

Creeley
calls me
a kind man

there are
those few
who agree

so I'm told

though I'm
not one to
agree

and all that
could change

when in
one week
someone
means
to be mean—

I change
my mind
being kind
because of it

No discretion
will do

trying to
be true to
what's said—

but a record
of one's
having lived

in one's time—

places

people

an untimely
but precise
intimacy

a clarity of mind—

and felt
for an instant
that pleasure

something to give

a place
one comes to

to listen

What's in a name
Who's that person, etc.

In and Out

As mind
is an edge
which opens
on the depth of
itself

Your hand
not your face
draws itself

             *

Must it be
whatever told to
you believe

One thinks
to know
but cannot
see

One deals the Tarot
unable to read it
precisely.

One coughs
spits
up blood
in the sink

One becomes irritable
careless in dress
One misses a day,
like they say

One gets a
new pair of
skates

slips on
the ice

One has a hard
time of it
at school—

attempts to
hang oneself

guilt shame violence

One sleeps late
wishing to
be rid of
these feelings

*

This fact of
feeling in oneself
for what one has
not become

the snow
falls

asleep

*

I feel form
as intimate presence

I want
it all

or not
at all

these   /
hands   /
       /   this
      /   face

so called
in words

What must it
feel
to crush
tenderness?

Whatever
could it

be
like

if not

what you
recognize
as being

     *

the tale of
the fox and
the burrow

to be suddenly exposed

a grove of
birch in
silent fog

You want
a place
to be
alone,

then be
alone
in it.

     *

The same
isn't you
or you
don't change

What way
now is not
precisely knowing
or not knowing

malevolence
auspiciously
withheld

one
by
one

the questions
answer themselves

to know
the difference

to begin
again

not darkness
not fear
not pain

the world is not
explained

It is a human
universe

*

Where we are
and were
and will
be

never
again

Where we are
and were and
will be

never again

RE WHO WE ARE WHO WE ARE WHO WE ARE WHO WE ARE WHO WE ARE WHO WE A

III

dal vero

Every year, the young girls come into flower on the beaches. They have only one season. The following year, they are replaced by other flowerlike faces which, the previous season, still belonged to little girls. For the man who looks at them, they are yearly waves whose weight and splendor break into foam over the yellow sand.

—Albert Camus,
Notebooks 1942-1951

*

. . . never run for a bus; there'll always be another.

—Meryl Streep,
Rolling Stone, 10/15/81

*

I have always regarded the neurotic as a failed artist.

—Otto Rank, *Art & Artist*

Little Italy

Thinking last night
capuccino   espresso

a walk thru dark streets
1   2   4:30 AM

time
tearing itself
apart

eyes fall to sleep

one mind one heart
at least

the city is waking

my own
sense of it, at least

Someone I've always
wanted to be—
me

seeing the girl
to the door

Thyself thou gavest, thy own worth then not knowing,
Or me, to whom thou gavest it, else mistaking

Sonnet 87, Shakespeare

This Will Kill That

A form of words takes shape
but in itself
is not complete

not simply given—

wants to say more
in saying less

proves nothing—

is of no help to me

what words—ennui, acedia

    dis-ease

    decomposition

    the infinity
    of death

    not *we*
    but a vital singularity

How shall one
say it,

that you
alone are you

a lovely
dignity

tenderness
disclosed as beauty

I want to kill this feeling in me
before it kills me
before it gets to me first

a walk of
half an hour
or so
thru city streets

one place in mind

all night awake

eyes   noses   feet

the alarm
goes off

You get up to
turn it off

and then go off

to sleep
again

night
comes
to
an end,
always

*

What is this fear of
unequivocal involvement

Why the death of something

Why not later

Why not never

*

"A Short
History
of Decay"

Think of the
implications

So much
has gone
away

Let's not
let it

Let it be otherwise

Let not the last time
be the first

Place it,
make a space
for it

one heart   one mind

It is now, of course, years later

Ananké

A place
to come back to
always

in the mind

one table
one dresser

one chair with a shirt
now hanging in front of it

stomach   hair   breast

curled up
in a kind of
close breathing

there is a time
elsewhere

disappearing

one window
adjacent to
the bed

the light
coming in

quietly

a dog
barking

The Enemies of Cold Water

The ambivalence—

you don't want
what you want

balance   ∞

clarity

passion

this fact of things

this *back* and *forth*
as the mind sees it

this and
that,

this—

and this
and that

sense of warmth

and hair hanging
hiding the face

and the one hand
finding the face

the last of your attributes

*

Sun again

window
comes into
focus

feet finally touching
from ceiling to floor

Being content

Being unsure—

again this ambivalence
this want and fear of
want

this repeated insistence

the risk involved
is not risk

or if it is
take it

That is,
the virtue of the mind

is that emotion

which causes
to see
of its own necessity

Heal yourself before attending to anything else.

—George Ohsawa

P h o t o g r a p h s   o f   A r c h i t e c t u r e

Words die of thirst when they are not understood
I said to ＿＿＿＿＿.

all is an act of courage

clarity

dignity

trust

a curtain caught in the breeze of an open window

rain coming in thru that same window

What happens when poems are not written

What happens when some play the game and win

What happens when we lie to ourselves

We tell ourselves there's so much time

We become victims of choice

We go thru life not knowing the miracle

99

what I know
is cold water
and I plunge
into it

> *The eyes*
> *have seen such*
> *beauty they close.*
>
> *But continue.*
>
> —Creeley,
> "Variations"

Briefe an Maxwell Perkins

You live the same life endlessly
or you can endlessly change your life

white showing
beneath the irises, the fact.

> you want to
> hurt and not
> get hurt:
>
> guilt   shame   violence

Time and place
to say
what hasn't as yet had chance to

night of rain

full moon

light before daybreak

knees
bared

wet
and wind
blown hair

all
those
things

one regards
as vain, sentimental

               —not so

The truth is as we find it

the deception that what we do
is more important than who
we are

the lie that you
can be beautiful

this
matter of
fact

this
and that
fear
inside us
changes

acts of courage

becoming sense of
touch

                                studies

                                perspectives

                                elevations

                                site plans   etc.

                                blues

                                browns

                                axonometrics   etc.

The form
insistent to
the fact
of things said

                            *

"The qualities of competition are selfish, brutal"
he says

                            *

                          Not far
                          from his office

from his office

someone
making
the bed

someone says,
jokingly

"you're
making
the bed
over you"

the ceiling

under the feet
the floor

knees standing
or bending

banging
the head

relating
the story:

What happens when you don't take notice
to the details of your life

What happens when the mundane shows itself
and you can't see it

What happens when you can neither deny nor live with
what you want

What happens when the imagination
is no longer essential

*

Passion, they said he had passion for the true,
for the intensely felt, the completely realized
(Maxwell Perkins and his authors)

*

Beauty
is too quick
for time

Thinking of Creeley—

*How that fact of
seeing someone you love away
from you in time will
disappear in time, too.*

How that fact of
seeing someone you love away
from you in time has not

convincing me
any combination of choices
will not do

"ambivalence"
you said

then as now

banging your head

this way, that—

feet
reaching

the ceiling

the floor

intelligence
defined

as beauty—

a kind of
beauty
transcending—

or not
at all

times before

the alarm goes off

the body drops
to the floor

cold shower

shampoo

shave

sharing
the same
toothbrush

cereal

cigarette

coffee

silence

out the door

the manic-
depressive
as such

begging to be slapped

the intelligent,
not the poor,
in spirit
as such

*

"Do not ever *defer* to my judgment"
he said
     in a letter to Scott

       *

    I keep coming back to you
    in my mind

    all those times

    past

    the pale
    forehead
    the same

    the eyes
    the same

    Max.

     Max

All Hallow's Eve

*for John, who first conveyed
the information*

The way
I heard
it was

*I didn't speak to you
the entire night at Kip's*

Your distance

my distance
from you

so that
there can't be
any way
to speak

attitudes
to sanctify
stupidity

vanity

neuroses

solicitation

not wanting
what you
want

victimized

not worthy

sense of
timing

hadn't
the
chance to

We have
in common
what we do
not share

What is said
or not said
finally

What
justification
can be used now

One cannot
return.

The past is
altered now.

I have
nothing
to give

having given
everything

the party's over

All the sick and sickly
instinctively strive
after a herd organization
as a means of shaking off
their dull displeasure
and feeling of weakness.

—Nietzsche, *Genealogy*
of Morals

Questions

All those
years
growing up

We're
better than
the world,

so *we suffer more*

you thought,

the myth.

What happens
when you use
your neuroses
as an excuse

instead of
getting
over them

What is
agreement of feeling
if you can't agree
on anything

What happens
when you count
on abuse
instead of kindness

when you
reciprocate
in like kind
as a test

acts of violence

wanting
others to feel
the way you
feel

in order
not to feel

What is
the purpose

What is accomplished

What is
the conclusion of
what possibilities
do exist for you
that you can't see

I hate similes

adjectives

expressions

to designate
the non-essential

Leopards
don't change
their spots,
a friend said, once

the cliché

and it was true to
my own experience
knowing you

briefly

I keep forgetting—
what you don't want
is what
you want, after all

desire, a word
you use loosely

or else,
something like
trust—

You reject it
you become angry

having felt
such pleasure
briefly

expecting
something else

aching
for
a fucking
bruise

to be *put down*

to be abused

strapped

strapped down to bed

stomach down
face down

spread-
eagled

rimmed

straddled

felched

welts, etc.

come
all
over

chest

stomach

face

Is that what
you like

the obvious
condition of
thought

of guilt

this ambivalence
met with
often enough
becomes a vanity, of sorts

pleasures of punishment

fulfilled

unfulfilled

jump on it

do it again

A sense of
self-disgust

self-dissatisfaction

rudeness

unreliability

lack of trust

Talking,

pointing out
the mistakes,

proves insufficient

What
you
don't like

that you like

What don't you
like

What
arouses guilt

in you

How to
be of use

how not to

be specific

Where is the so-called
heightened awareness
of individual
identity

Where
is the
loveliness

the
mind
feeling

fuck *the heart*

Where do you go
from here
if *here's* not
where you are

where do you
put your feet
down? What to do
with hands

the questions
you keep asking
yourself: *Who
am I? Where do
I belong?*

*Where will I be
ten years hence*

repeatedly,

the fact.

Where will you . . .?

You sleep
you get up

What do you
think
you do
all day

You live
the same
life endlessly—

how not to change

not knowing
how to

or else
how not to

knowing how to

not wanting to

impatient
with yourself

all
these
things

What is
the next breath
you take

What is the last one

What is the one
after that

and the
one after that
one

What do you mean
to say
when you
face me

when you
do

not saying a word
I had not already
heard before

Where is
the coherence

the continuity

the dependability
of response

Where is
the intelligence

clarity of mind

What hadn't you
discovered—

misdirected
intentions

not come to
terms with—

What is recovered
to be of use, finally

Some way

some
instance or other

does exist

to say
what *must*
be said

beyond
whatever
purpose
proves
sufficient

All the things
we think of
will come true:

old age
sickness
death

I don't love you
anymore, I thought,
suddenly

and was relieved

Nonetheless

you are here,

not in any
real sense
that is
comforting.

What we
can't get back
that's lost,

is lost

is irreversible

unconnected

What is observed

what is thought
felt and proved
finally

is of value—

that
things grow

give
presence to

my life

persons, also
are
of value

Memories of
what will happen,
happen

not now

but later

Who uses me
is whom I use

To the Future

Are you someone
you want to be,
finally

the choices you make
to get there

Careers are for fools,
a friend said

         *

Role-playing

You hurt yourself
to get what you want

to be rescued—

then to
refuse to

this matter of choice

         *

Abuse me is what you beg for

If no one else will—
whip yourself

I don't own
what you

do to yourself,

to feel *not ok*

2 6:v i i:79 n y c

Feelings
don't
stay the same
ever

or Creeley
saying something abt

love
disappears
in time, too.

Or simply changes.

Like today, for instance,
walking 14th Street,

this is
the address
François
lived at—

and five
days later,

an open space
between The Palladium
the Gramercy Gym

Angus telling me,
but no—

       his death, then

at 41, Kathmandu

        not much else
        to go on—

Personal history

or

what stays
in the
mind:

Little Italy

streets of rain
reflected lights

the six
flights of
stair

love in a loft
bed

dream

dog barking

getting up with the sun

the sound of running water

breakfast, and "grace to be born . . .", etc.

e n v o i

"—only
claim

to
fame—

taking
Bryan

to the
laundry"

a
friend
says.

And of my
poems to her

wch will
have avenged

Bryan.

3:ix:80 nyc

IV

THIS WILL KILL THAT

An experiment in autobiography

. . . It is the woman's part: be it lying, note it,
The woman's; flattering, hers; deceiving, hers;
Lust and rank thoughts, hers, hers; revenges, hers;
Ambitions, covetings, change of prides, disdain,
Nice longing, slanders, mutability,
All faults that name, nay, that hell knows,
Why hers, in part, or all; but rather all;
For even to vice
They are not constant, but are changing still:
One vice, but of a minute old, for one
Not half so old as that. I'll write against them,
Detest them, curse them: yet 'tis greater skill
In a true hate to pray they have their will:
The very devils cannot plague them better.

—Posthumus speaking,
Cymbeline, Shakespeare

. . . as the Italian proverb says—"Revenge is a dish which people of taste prefer to eat cold."

—"Kind Hearts and Coronets"

In those days, he who was born a poet became an architect.

—Victor Hugo,
Notre-Dame de Paris

This Will Kill That

It is my belief that there are no wise men in a wise nation. An honest man is blissfully unaware of his virtue. A man who is healthy does not know what health is. The innocent person does not recognize his own innocence. If you think you possess honesty, justice, patience, health, you are apt to be a stranger to these virtues.

I receive letters from friends and persons I've never met who thank me. These letters pile up on my desk. They come on days sometimes that find me in a state of deep depression. I am saved. Letters give the sense of where happily other human beings are in relation to me. They have ideas about me that I don't have. That I am "generous," "courageous," "mysterious," "patient," "enigmatic"—I reject these epithets. Not that I underestimate the pleasure I have felt from such letters. I don't have the ego to admit these qualities nor the modesty to deny them. The good opinion of others, even in cases where I do not share it, is still useful to me or promises to become so. To become what one is, one must not have the faintest notion of *what* one is, nor have the pride to know it. We become only that which we are innately.

*   *   *   *   *

The artist must possess something in order to *be* something; in the artist-type, according to Otto Rank, the creative urge is constantly related, ideologically, to his own ego, or at any rate this is so in a higher degree and fuller measure than in the average man, so that one cay say of the artist that he does not practice his calling, but *is* it (represents it ideologically). The artist must live his ideology so that he, as well as others, believes it is true. This ideological experience acts both as a means to make artistic productivity possible and as a means to live a real life. He in his desire to protect his integrity and his spirit from the misunderstanding and insensitivity of others, must love and be proud of the work he does in the quiet determination of what he values. For the artist, therefore, his calling is not a means of livelihood, but life itself.

133

* * * * *   .

To live is to create. And to love is to live. The eagerness to love, suppressed, is a refusal to live. Happiness or misery in the apparent world is the result of a multitude of daily decisions. And through decisions everything that happens provides some experience or develops some quality in character that has been hidden or missing. To *see* what is hidden or missing one must postpone judgment. The inability to resist judgment comes from regression, inhibition, pressure, tension. The effect of these neuroses is *Sanpaku*, not only an illness of the body but a dangerous condition of the spirit and psyche, a repressed violence evidenced in the eye: perpendicular poise missing in mind and body which are without center of gravity. Lack of vitality, lack of composure. The dangers are great; the probability that one will come to grief and perish is tremendous.

One loses entirely the capacity to think for oneself. A state of ambivalence. One enters a kind of chaos of neurosis. A confusion of discordant parts. Yet vanity sees advantage in neurosis, which in turn becomes one's own vanity, so that a conscious stupidity is perpetrated—*bêtise bourgeoise*—which claims that neurosis is a beneficial condition, a paradigm of authentic existence and cognition. Every vanity inclines towards stupidity; a refusal to let things approach; a state of defense and fear against what is truly beneficial, against that which one really wants and is afraid to want. To avoid hurt, one stops wanting.

She represents a contradiction of values: she sits on the floor between two chairs; she says Yes and No in the same breath, finding herself unable to act. Every decision, no matter how trivial, becomes an agony. She forces the spirit to recognize things against its inclination and often against the wishes of the heart. She punishes herself. A neurotic sensibility does not understand its frequent feelings of displeasure but believes them justified in determining destiny. *I don't want what I want* makes clear the guilt of knowing and fearing what she wants and therefore denying herself what she wants. One must know what one wants: *nosce te ipsum*.

134

When she can no longer think for herself, this is psychological regression and decadence—a deterioration of the spirit: revenging herself against life. Punishment does not expiate; what is done is not undone—the desire to hurt and not get hurt: a drop of cruelty to be tested, to raise cruelty to a respectability. To force someone to retaliate with cruel acts is nothing more than aggression. The conscious act of *to hurt and not get hurt* masks an unconscious desire to want to be hurt. This behavior is symptomatic of the sado-masochistic type. In short, she is always both the torturer and the tortured, deriving satisfaction from being degraded as well as from degrading herself. I know such individuals *so well* that I become weary. They are sneaky, timid, and cosmopolitan; they pretend modesty, reducing themselves to such a state of psychological self-violation that their presence arouses nausea. ("Heal yourself before attending to anything else." —George Ohsawa.)

* * * * *

She is uneasy with fear and asks how she should relate in conversation and action to a person who attracts her. Her longing for the lover to be only a friend betrays her: wanting to approve of only one part of the lover's qualities and wishing to abolish the others, to neutralize him, to eliminate his magic. The relationship consists in following up the stupidity or folly as fast as possible with some good sense. Goodwill gives insight.

To have insight is to be always conscious of all the aspects under which any event can be considered. Of what avail is knowledge with no insight to integrate that knowledge? The man of insight must not only love his enemies, he must also be able to hate his friends.

Freud sets limits for the kinds of relationships that are possible between human beings. He himself found an intimate friend and a hated enemy indispensable to his emotional life; he said that he always created them anew if they temporarily did not exist; sometimes they coincided in the same person. More than once he turned a close friend into an enemy. We may agree that to love our enemies is both important and difficult, but few of us have many chances to love the enemies we have.

Love is an expression of the ego; for anyone who wants and gets something in return—perhaps something of himself in return for something given of himself—knows love is above all sentiments the most egotistic and often difficult, and when wounded the least generous. I would be useless if I could not accept; I would be useless if someone did not want something of me. I do not give in order to receive; but whoever cannot give, receives nothing. To give is to become a creator.

All high creation in art is committed and passional: risks itself, for there is no art where there is nothing to overcome. Having the temperament of a man of action, one instinctively chooses what is dangerous, for danger challenges curiosity about the degree of one's strength and courage. Nietzsche points out, "One lives for the day, one lives very fast, one lives irresponsibly: this is called 'freedom' . . . the free man is a warrior."

History and moral philosophy are ineffectual to teach the man of action and the warrior. History tells us only what has been, poetry what should be; moral philosophy is dry analysis—a symptom of decadence; poetry motivates to emulation and action.

language as the act of the instant

*

the habits of thought are the habits of action

—Charles Olson

Freedom can also be found, from my experience, through discipline and patience: to wait and to prepare oneself. A truly creative person is more truly sane because he is disciplined and patient; the pseudo-romantic view of mad genius is a myth and no longer viable. But those partisans of art who still insist on explaining artistic genius by means of psychic imbalance are capitulating to the once dominant view which held that creative genius was not free from neurosis.

As Lionel Trilling says in his essay "Art and Neurosis", ". . . the rich complexity which his ego is doomed to control is not the definition of the artist's genius, for we can by no means say that the artist is pre-eminent in the rich complexity of elements in conflict within him. The slightest acquaintance with the clinical literature of psychoanalysis will suggest that a rich complexity of struggling elements is no uncommon possession. And that same literature will make it abundantly clear that the devices of art—the most extreme devices of poetry, for example—are not particular to the mind of the artist but are characteristic of the mind itself." As Freud says in a passage which follows close on a Trilling quotation elsewhere, "The neurotic symptoms are activities which are detrimental, or at least useless, to life as a whole; the person concerned frequently complains of them as obnoxious to him for they involve suffering and distress for him. The principal injury they inflict lies in the expense of energy they entail, and, besides this, in the energy needed to combat them. Where the symptoms are extensively developed, these two kinds of effort may exact such a price that the person suffers a very serious impoverishment in available mental energy which consequently disables him for all the important tasks of life. This result depends principally upon the amount of energy taken up in this way; therefore you will see that 'illness' is essentially a practical conception. But if you look at the matter from a theoretical point of view and ignore this question of degree, you can very well see that we are all ill, i.e., neurotic; for the conditions required for symptom-formation are demonstrable also in normal persons."*

I have cited Freud's statement of the essential sickness of the psyche only because it stands as the refutation of what is implied by the more common literary use of the theory of neurosis to account for

---

* This account can be found fully and in similar translation by James Strachey in Lecture XXII—"The Paths to the Formation of Symptoms" from *Introductory Lectures on Psychoanalysis.*

genius. The real meaning of artistic genius lies in what Lionel Trilling calls "distinguished ability, rather than in the sense it later came to have, that of a unique power, an originating power, which puts the person who possesses it into a class apart." Genius thus refers to faculties of perception, representation and realization, and in these terms alone, and not necessarily referring to neurotic tendency.

What sets the artistic genius apart from the simply neurotic who has pretensions to approximate or acquire the character of the artist by merely planning or even attempting to work as the artist does, is that which gives the artist-type his individuality and power to conceive, plan, and work, and bring his work to a conclusion, realizing his potential to an unusual degree. This I feel to be the condition Richard Aldington defines in his Introduction to D. H. Lawrence's *Apocalypse:* "Like every creative man, Lawrence suffered from the hundreds of people who would like to create, and can't. The unconscious envy of this type disguises itself as 'critical standards', and its attack is always against the essentially creative and original artist."

Mediocrity has no greater consolation than in the thought that genius is not immortal.

—Goethe

It is not uncommon in our society for certain kinds of neurotic people to imitate the artist in his lifestyle. They follow the artist in everything except successful performance. They are only half-artists, and half-artists are merely skillful philistine imitators whose value Coleridge compared to that of spitting over a bridge. They are false, partial, narrow, commonplace and divisive. They ape genius and they perpetuate alienation. They procrastinate; they are afraid to fail and, therefore, afraid to try. To avoid failure, they stop trying. Otto Rank, in *Art and Artist*, points out that he has always regarded the neurotic as a "failed artist."

Genius is its own end, and draws its means and the style of its

138

architecture not from talent alone but inner perception. It is the combined ability to become a child again at will, to utilize a child's perceptual intuition of time and space, and to maintain sanity, perspective, buoyancy, to see through the show of things into things. This is the objectivity that Matthew Arnold spoke of, the effort "to see the object as in itself it really is." And seeing things as they are, the child apprehends the reality of what is positive and embraces that. Thus the child becomes a discriminating optimist. Genius is not a form of neurosis. It is a normal manifestation. The eighteenth century did not find the artistic genius to be less or more than other men, and certainly the Renaissance did not.

*　　*　　*　　*　　*

The spiritual combat is more bloody than any human battle.

—Arthur Rimbaud

It is not enough for a genius to be an active hero. Neither the courage nor the gift suffices. The heroic ideal and the heroic ordeal both require recognition to some extent; there must be a thirst for resistance and opponents—enemies that are his equals; there must be hydras and dragons and minotaurs and myopic gods with whom to enter into single combat, to wrestle, throw down, wage war for his thoughts—the concept of feeling the struggle. "What is heroic," says John Cage, "is to accept the situation in which you find yourself." Who will permit me entrance into their caves, hideouts, and labyrinths? Who will give me the necessary strength? Where is the love that will support such a venture? Who will inspire it?

On the one hand we have the godlike hero, in the epic sense, who announces and demonstrates himself, wants power to do great deeds and win glory, appears to suffer nothing and succeeds in everything, sleeps with the most beautiful girls, and yearns to be eternally twenty. He doesn't want any one thing, he wants to experience *everything*, to prefer danger to comfort, or possible death as something that he himself wills and for which he takes responsibility.

His path is strewn with tricks of the gods and oceans to be crossed. There is another kind of hero who has other aims; neither heroicized nor sentimental. He expresses his inward autonomy paradoxically. He does not act in any extraordinary way; but appears from the outside to be normal.

*　　*　　*　　*　　*

What would we be if we knew nothing of wrath, revenge, scorn, cunning, and violence? What are we before we make something of ourselves? What can we acquire but what we are? Would there be happiness if we did not experience courage and freedom in the presence of another?

> *There are men*
> *　　who as they live*
> *　　　　fling caution to the*
> *wind and women praise them*
> *　　and love them for it.*

—William Carlos Williams

How cheerful to have a common experience and shared enthusiasm; but whoever loves another cannot will that person to love him in return.* I don't want to carry a glass of water across the desert to see a thirsty person knock the glass out of my hand. Our greatest efforts to please are often met with the least success.

---

* In Freud's view this sexual incongruity produces a domestic tragedy: man loves a woman who cannot love him in return. But a man can assuage his disappointment with the knowledge that he has already surrendered his narcissism to her and is therefore feeling morally superior to the woman who scorns him.

As in one lifetime there are only limited ways of expression, so in any relationship only certain ranges of mutual love are realized. The poet is reminded that the "higher love" found in literature is a rationalization of those who are impotent in the "lower love" of real life. The poet feels the need to reach for the unattainable and change the solid world of facts into the kingdom of his dreams. His activity may be termed antisocial, since it could irritate his fellow men and make their happiness suspect to themselves. But the poet's ambition to elevate mankind, his dissatisfaction with the flatness of life as it is, are only the results of his misanthropic disposition.

There is contrast between Proust's lack of faith and Dante's faith in the possibilities of human intimacy. Proust believed that the more we love a person the less we understand and respect that person; Dante that the greater our love of someone, the greater our understanding. To Dante increased knowledge was love, love knowledge—pedagogic, in a sense. For Proust, as for Freud, time eventually destroys love; for Dante time increases love. Love can become an intensification of seeing, a looking into hidden possibilities. Freud's view that almost every love is closely allied to hostility not only agrees with Schopenhauer's view, but with Proust who believed that intimacy breeds contempt.

> *and each reason for love always*
> *a certain hostility . . .*

> —Frank O'Hara

*   *   *   *   *

What Mondrian called "equilibrated relationships" are as fundamental to people as to architecture. Balance is all-important: a person should be capable of being scrutinized from no matter how unexpected an angle without being caught in a disequilibrated relationship. Where one person refuses to accept the reality of the other the relationship is doomed; communication breaks down.

She refuses an intimacy as if she waited for some better intimacy to come. She surrounds herself with an ever increasing number of substitutes for genuine feeling. She does not even have to be clear in her own mind what it is she wants. It's possible that at a particular moment she cannot share the desire for any of the physical sensations which might otherwise delight her, because of the attitude *I don't want what I want*, and is smug to the point of justifying this position. The sheer human perverseness, the willfulness of her attitude, is astonishing. Freud calls this "a psychical conflict." One part of the personality champions certain wishes while another part opposes them and fends them off. Without such conflict there is no neurosis.

Robert Creeley expressed the nature of such ambivalence in several poems:

> Do you think that if
> you once do what you want
> to do you will want not to do it.
>
> ["Do You Think. . ."]

*

>   you
> want so
>
> much so
> little.
>
> ["The Language"]

*

> All you say you want
> to do to yourself you do
> to someone else as yourself. . .
>
> ["Anger"]

*   *   *   *   *

She hates herself for her indecisions—a hatred so fierce that she's helpless against it and may psychically destroy herself. She does not hate herself because she is worthless but because she is driven to reach beyond herself. The hatred results from the discrepancy between *what I would be* and *what I am*. She becomes vain about her neurosis, preventing her from functioning as she should, either totally or in some particular area of life. The recognition of any necessity applying to herself would pull her down from her lofty world into actuality, where she would be subject to the same natural laws as anybody else. And it is this need to eliminate necessity from her life which turns into the claim of not wanting to have her needs met—namely to love or be loved. She defends herself against such feelings with involuntary mistrust. She lives in a perpetual state of anxiety. She wants to be less vulnerable, less in need of love, and not condemned to disappointment: the dominant condition being the incapability of believing in herself. She shuts herself off from life around her. She becomes paranoid, hostile. She unconsciously gives up some pleasure or power, inflicts pain on herself in order to secure some other power or some other pleasure. She doesn't have the honesty to admit that she is committing an act of self-violation, and yet she is seized by disgust with herself. To get what she wants she sets herself up to get hurt. Abruptly she plunges into opposite valuations. She feels attracted to what harms her; self-destruction is turned into a sign of value. For stimulation she gets pleasure from the consciousness of hurting someone—in order to get hurt.

Fearing to be attacked she attacks first—those who had no intention of attacking her. Having been predisposed by a family situation to certain mental and emotional incidents in youth, she now invites injury in the wish to identify with a father or mother, who had been similarly injured by each other.

> *Some,*
> *fearing the example of their parents, are*
> *afraid to love   .   others fearing*

the example of their parents,

are helpless before the emotion, not
believing it possible.

—Paul Blackburn ["Here They Go"]

A lack of trust becomes evident: someone wants something from her. She feels guilty for having money, she disguises the fact that she lives off the interest of inherited wealth. She pretends *living on the edge.* She experiences herself as poor, impoverished and expresses delusions of poverty. She hates what she has because she feels that it is not having; it does not belong to her. Out of guilt she finds some kind of work into which she plunges with selfless devotion to give her a goal. What goal? She wants to prove something, with a compulsiveness of wanting more in order to *become* more, to impose herself on others, to express herself, even at the cost of her well-being. There is already a hint of the despair so characteristic of people who have, or think they have, everything.

She doesn't realize that trying to become "someone" aims at *nothing* and achieves *nothing.* A goal, modest or grandiose, is set by ambition: a desire to be more than what she is. In her career she may show all the earmarks of neurotic ambition. She wants to acquire and keep hold and accumulate, to set precedents and secure advantage. She must continually perform mental gymnastics to keep herself convinced that she is living up to her idealized image, that she is, indeed, a superior being. She rejects herself out of a desire to act a role contrary to herself. In any conflict between what she is and what she wants to be, she acts the part of what she wants to be. She has pretensions: she wishes and attempts things beyond her powers. It is nothing more than a striving for power and more power; it is nothing more than calculated ambition. She pretends she receives a salary by calling the work she does "a job": she lies by omission. She resents reality for not being some fairy-tale compensation of itself—different from what, in fact, it is. Her vanity drives her to resemble others in needs and demands. Another seduction is conducted under the mask of altruism, which in itself is a specific form of egoism that appears under certain psychological conditions. Neurotic pride, in all its forms, is false pride.

In every experience she wishes to move ahead, to actualize her possibilities; but at the same time she plays with the prospect of not doing so—i.e., with a wish to negate them. It is the shrinking of one's world. She suffers from the fact that she cannot or will not accept herself, her individuality, her ability to be and to grow, hence such complaints as "I can't accomplish anything, I can't succeed in anything."

She criticizes herself to excess, which means that she makes too great demands on her potential, so that failing to attain leads only to more self-criticism. She keeps saying: *others must not do better than me.* Excellent work is not enough, it must be the absolute best.

She suffers from acute penis-envy. Unable to resolve her penis-envy she attempts a "flight from womanhood" by developing a neurotically driven, competitive, aggressive personality. She thus attempts to deny her absence of a penis by adopting those behaviors traditionally associated with males. She adopts a selective and feminine behavior as a disguise for her deep-seeded, intense hatred of men, which leads her to act in a castrating manner once the man's attention has been gained. Consequently, sexual responsiveness and pleasure are denied. In doing so, she "pretends" to be self-sufficient strategically, in order to be able to continue to charm and conquer men.

For Rene Girard, the woman "is no more self-sufficient than the man who desires her . . . but the success of her strategy allows her to keep up the appearance of it by offering to herself as well a desire she can copy. If desire for her is precious to her, it is because it supplies the necessary sustenance for a false self-sufficiency which would fall apart were she totally deprived of admiration."

Comparing this thwarted type with the artist, it is clear that the artist is the antithesis of the self-critical neurotic type. By the intensity of such self-reproach, neurotics try to prove how high their standards are, and therefore how really superior they are. Not that the artist does not criticize himself, but by accepting his personality he not only fulfills what the neurotic is striving for in vain, but goes far beyond it. Neurosis is not so much a wound as an activity with a purpose, a particular kind of activity, a *conflict*. Some self-created conflicts come from the mere wish to make oneself interesting; but whereas the artist masters these conflicts, in form and content, by giving them aesthetic shape, the neurotic fails to do so. It has become fashionable to give credence to the idea that neurotic conflicts constitute a productive-creative force; but in "Art and Neurosis," Trilling takes his stand on the side of art stripped of neurotic tendencies. He disputes the popular idea, which is also advanced by Edmund Wilson in *The Wound and the Bow* [1941], that the artist's neurosis is responsible for his art. Yet it is not enough to say that a neurotic's weaknesses do not impair his ability to create. It is not even sufficient to say that they are often the stuff out of which genuine art is made. Psychopathology can in no way be claimed a prerequisite, or even a manifestation, of the creative process. It is characteristic of the healthy artist to be able to sustain conflict and doubt with little or no anxiety that would be paralyzing. The ability to live with what is possible is one test of being healthy and creative. Insight is health.

What I am saying is that a work of art in whose genesis a neurotic element may be found is therefore irrelevant or diminished in value. That the effectiveness of any artist does not depend on some behavioral/physiological characteristic. Rather, what distinguishes the artist from the neurotic is his power to shape the material of pain or other experience that we all have and in the process to sacrifice, without fearing loss of power, that part of life and experience which makes art of them.

"For when he creates," says Otto Rank, "the artist uses the whole of himself without being in danger of losing that self therein, for it is certain that the work itself, from his point of view, represents only a part of his ego, although it does in fact represent the whole artist and his personality. The artist does not go charily with his life, like the neurotic, but positively spends it as he creates. The artist is still one who, by virtue of what he is in his own nature, reacts in a special way to all human experience," whereas the neurotic feels safer to restrict his/her life, tending to regard the possibility of being carried away into the fantastic as a danger to be avoided. Kierkegaard would describe the difference between the healthy and neurotic state thus: that the artist moves ahead despite the conflict, actualizing his freedom with regard to his own will, while the unhealthy person retrenches to a "shut-in" condition, sacrificing his freedom.

What was once the whole of the artist's life, has become to an increasing extent, merely the background of life. What would have been an extraordinary question a hundred years ago is now current: "Yes, you earn a living, you support a family, you love and hate, but what else do you do?" She measures her esteem of herself by what she does, and not by what she is. She has not learned the lie: that what she does is more important than who she is, the lie of wishing *not* to see what and how she does see. It is a lie she thinks necessary to achieve her goals. The difference between healthy strivings and neurotic drives for glory is one between spontaneity and compulsion. Perhaps she has no words to express emotions about something so tremendous as deception. Nevertheless, she actively participates in the neurotic process, functions, so to speak, according to it, and in ways that sustain and are indispensable in making the characteristic neurotic experiences inevitable, however discomforting they may be.*

Everything is unrest, disturbance, doubt, abandoned attempts. She prepares for guilt feelings in order to feel *guilt* rather than to feel bad for no reason. Her drive to be satisfied is expressed in dissatisfaction with the present state of things. It is not whether she is content with herself, but whether she is content with anything at all. A frightful

---

* This corresponds to what Freud said in Lecture XXIV, "The Common Neurotic State" (from *Introductory Lectures on Psychoanalysis*): ". . . whenever a neurotic is faced by a conflict he takes flight into illness." This phrase appeared first in Freud's paper "Some General Remarks on Hysterical Attacks" (1909) where some further references will be found.

lassitude. She chain-smokes. She complains of nervousness, she invariably fears that she will lose her feminine attractiveness, and yet she presents a sloppy appearance before intimate friends. She takes on a waif-like little-lost-girl appearance. She experiences herself primarily as a victim, if only to protect herself from the truths that might expose her to the ambiguities of the world. She makes the other her victim, only partially out of envy or animosity; but also out of fear and greed, a desire for safety, and a desire for personal authority beyond all question.

She hates not being the wonderful person she would like to be. Feeling unacceptable to herself—indeed hateworthy or contemptible—she cannot possibly believe that anybody else could love her, and must necessarily be suspicious of any declaration of love.* She punishes the body—a most personal possession—and her ego. She feels inferior: her self-esteem suffers. She needs someone to use her up. She seeks out those who pretend to have answers—analysts to flatter her, make her forget, overcome stupidities, and blot out her past.

. . . the neurotic person will try to make the past nonexistent.

—Sigmund Freud

But past who can recall, or done undo.

—John Milton, "Paradise Lost"

---

* Henry Harper Hart, in discussing "Extreme Narcissism," made a similar observation: "Extreme narcissism," writes Hart, "implies weakness and vulnerability. Insecure persons inflate themselves with self-love to compensate for a lack of devotion from without and because of an unconscious feeling of not deserving it."

148

This miserable flattery for personal vanity! Her gratitude consists in misunderstanding. She pays science to understand her. And this in itself acquires a kind of sanction.

Can she realize her true nature? And what ultimately does she know of herself? What and whom does she deny or accept? What has happened, at bottom? What is achieved? Has she "turned out well," as they say? That people should deceive themselves as to their own needs does not surprise me. It's not that I mistrust psychoanalysts; but all my instincts are antagonized by a person volunteering information, or boasting, of being taken into analysis. Here begins my nausea.

Though she is active, she so often produces nothing. She feels restricted as to possibilities of expression. She devotes herself more and more to abstractions to avoid the frustration of not completing artistic enterprises. She never fulfills the work she imagines in her; never realizes the secret splendor of her intentions . . . doesn't really get there. She lives in her miscreations and blames circumstance or fate for what she brings on herself. She constantly attributes her shortcomings to others. She squanders her capabilities and feelings. She squanders what is most precious—the spirit. And tomorrow she knows no more than she did yesterday how she might be helped.

*   *   *   *   *

One who loves passionately is cured of love in the end.

—Chinese proverb

My thought is that what could separate two people most profoundly is profound love. The fact remains: not that one fears the other but that one fears the love the other truly has; because it somehow is destined to succeed.

The love that should reshape and elevate the beloved: *growth*, in a word—or, actually, the *feeling* of growth. Richness of personality;

abundance in oneself, overflowing and bestowing; instinctive good health; and self-affirmation: these produce great love. One seems to oneself transfigured, stronger, richer, more perfect. There can be no excess of love, of knowledge, of beauty, when these attributes are considered in the purest sense. Profound love affirms an optimism. But *What begins*, ends.

⋆   ⋆   ⋆   ⋆   ⋆

It is the artist who interprets himself and everyone around him in some medium that corresponds to the intricacy of his existence—a medium that does not deceive or make a fool of him, nor betray him in the end. The artist must believe in his medium, that it says something about action or passion, and adds meaning without merely copying nature. But when he uses his medium, without passion and without acknowledging nature, the work grows thin. There is no greater sin against two of our art media—architecture and poetry—the last bastions of pure expression—nothing more contemptible than to use artistic license as a specious cover for misunderstanding what architecture and poetry are: knowledge. And this knowledge bears directly upon the human experience.

Most architecture reveals an appalling lack of consideration of the human element. Architecture can only have an abiding integrity if it resides in harmony with its time, setting, and function; but it no longer works with the wholeness that it once had because it now relies on a bureaucratic complexity—which is also evident to some degree in the certification of poets with MFAs. All the magic, all the inspiration, are suppressed. One's passional impulses are murdered; intellectual and spiritual integrity violated. The Masters program in poetry is a classic example of manufacturing credentials for the specialized degrees published poets can do without. The life of an epoch is expressed by the art of that epoch. Where architecture and poetry are vulgarized, there the life of the people is also essentially vulgar in emotional quality.

Good art is relatively uncommon and depends on the quality of the artist's character expressed in the work. Confucius believed that the

150

nastiness in a man's character would damage his art. Likewise William Carlos Williams finds parallel:

> The Poet himself,
> > what does he think of himself
> > > facing his world?
> It will not do to say,
> > as he is inclined to say:
> > > Not much. The poem
> would be in *that* betrayed.

* * * *

> The poet
> > cannot slight himself
> without slighting
> > his poem. . .

—William Carlos Williams, "The Pink Locust"

But what appears to be an advance in art does not mean an advance in values. If man's worth cannot keep pace with his intellectual and technological development, all his progress will prove self-destructive. Technology creates no values. The best it can do is provide new ways and opportunities through which values express themselves, and if these means do not further that end, then technology becomes not a blessing, but a curse.

Architecture's rebirth can be expected only when the *essence* of language, thought, vision, has been rediscovered through personal relationships: the building spirit that builds under the most unfavorable conditions. What's needed for the future is to break away from tradition in an attempt to avoid producing derivative work both in architecture and poetry. If the expression is stale or false, so is the artist's intelligence.

* * * * *

151

The highest concept of the architecure of the poem came to me from Robert Creeley: "FORM is never more than an extension of CONTENT," since—as he also makes clear—"the point is that no form can exist as a possibility apart from that which informs it, the content of which it is the issue." Nowhere else does one have this intellectual passion in statements of form—as to the power of form, the will to accept form through language as a maximal state: namely, *proprioception*—"sensibility within the organism by movement of its own tissues" [Olson]. Content and form become equal in the order of time, but in the order of genesis content is prior to form. Content possesses the capacity of initiating form. Louis H. Sullivan's famous principle of architecture, "Form follows function" can be translated into *form follows purpose*. The theme of a poem or a novel or a cathedral defines its purpose.

*   *   *   *   *

The desire to know what *is* calls forth that other desire: *thus it ought to be*. For the knowledge of *thus it ought to be* is a consequence of the question: *How is the progression possible?* The disagreement between our desires and the course of our lives tells us that *thus it ought to be* is our wish to overcome what *is*. This insistence on an imaginary condition betrays human life when it substitutes ideal ends for real ends.

I'm aware of *what might be*, taking into account *what is*, in whatever I set out to do—to sift through and express the *thing* experienced, to bring into language an architectural form which is an ultimate simplicity. Not what the poet idealizes but what he *is* for those who are not poets, gives him his intrinsic value. He provokes and awakens the needs in others which he alone can provide for. Because he is aware of what happens to him and to others, he prides himself on telling the truth. By doing his work honestly and with purpose he unfolds himself. The poet's value is exceptional in his care for the inventory of human experiences. The experiences that he records correspond closely with what others have always felt and thought, and yet may not know how to analyze, even for themselves. His poetry not only commits the poet to the kind of voice he has and to the mode of writing he develops, it also *defines* him as one others respond to. This intrinsic relationship of language to the social value of commitment and uttered truth is strategic for support of his ego development.

*   *   *   *   *

I respect myself: everything else follows from that. I look inside myself. I feel instinctively sure of myself in relation to another. I do not yield to the subconscious, I am informed by it. I believe in impulse, energy, vision. I do not believe in guilt, shame, or shamelessness. I am dialectical, ideological, subversive, voyeuristic. I am an eroticist. I am a sensualist. I am superstitious. I am a provoker and an energizer. My life contains hundreds of follies. Therefore I am not to be trusted. My actions which turn against me may, artistically considered, be nonetheless useful. I understand how to fight my way through, to endure, to turn circumstances to my own benefit. The truer I am to myself, the more distinctive will be my work. I never write anything I do not actually experience firsthand. Every man has this call to do something unique. All human actions, as Ayn Rand points out, are goal-directed, consciously or subconsciously; for purposelessness is contrary to man's nature and is a state of neurosis.

*   *   *   *   *

I come to terms with myself, with others. I do not bear a grudge; yet I carry a lash. I am always the first to want to "clear the boards," so to speak, but on my own terms. I make use of acquired knowledge; I capitalize on experience. I have taken what I find most suitable for my own wants and made it mine by building upon the best of what I have observed, thought, felt, and absorbed finally, and as of value to me in the welter. I am the opposite of the neurotic because I know how to accept myself.

I welcome those periods when I'm not creating. I never feel pressed for time. This space and time reinforces the space and time when I do produce a *work.* I trust my perceptions. I know how to find my way back from the world of the imagination and, to quote Freud, "once more get a firm foothold in reality." I am often mistaken for an easy optimist. Not so. I am patient. I am discriminating. My persevering optimism allows me to breathe, to gather strength. It reminds me that I can make choices.

I conceal myself in the presence of the unfamiliar. Yet I can be intimate and accessible without giving myself entirely away. Surprise involves disappearance—also a divine principle described by the Hindus. I try to keep my past at a distance. I don't want to waste but to liberate myself with each experience. I don't want to be picturesque. I try to avoid a high profile. They tell me I look like a poet. I am chameleon-like: I change my appearance at will, often to make recognition difficult. I am aware that I arouse fear, that I have the capacity to intimidate, though not meaning to. I sometimes find myself in the precarious and dangerous situation of being admired and despised by people who have never met me. Even my name evokes reaction.

The liveliness of my temperament keeps me from being understood and is used against me. I welcome having opponents so long as they are strong opponents. But I curtail their possible mischief when I can. I stand in simple relation to individuals, to friends and strangers alike. I honor them by recognizing, by choosing, by admitting them. I conserve myself. I make no promises. Yet responsibility increases. I don't want to fall short of my own standards.

I regard rejection as a guarantee of something better, always presupposing no lack of those with whom one may communicate. Something always develops. There is no fixed home to be found, and no permanent relationships. I have no idea of what's going to happen, or where the joy or pain will be should either occur. Whatever encounter is made always returns according to the law of "eternal recurrence," insofar as every moment has its logic in a sequence. That everything recurs substantiates Einstein's principle that energy is not lost; it only changes.

What seems inevitable interests me. And for me love and good are inevitable. I have never been out of love with anyone who embraces the whole of life without fear or favor. Only those who change and move with me into the future remain related to me in some way, those who do not I invent poems as a hell. My art is a revenge, a memory of overcoming a difficult fate by imposing its form upon those who frustrate me.

This invention of hell, for one's enemies.

—Ezra Pound

*

The insolence of the poem is the expression of a reflex reaction.

—Jean-Paul Sartre

I write from antagonism, as well as from love. I believe that to be a poet is to create one's own psychic phenomena and establish them in conscious reality. My poems are based on what my lifestyle determines, but only to the degree of correspondence between my perceptions of the actual world of persons and things. My whole way of living the true dreams and dramas of the life I am destined for is a continuous justification of my impulse to create and is the material expressed ideologically in my writing.

Experience is a movement of consciousness from one situation to another, in the course of which the self "creates" experience from nothing. A moment of experience is known primarily through the senses; it is physical, and its physicality is indispensible to its symbolic uses on the level of eternity. The imagery of earthly beauty acquires a value only when it is seen from the perspective of eternity.

I hoard experiences. Experience teaches only the teachable. I cannot unlearn anything but in fact learn more and more. Things always seem to get better; but why had I been writing poems about relationships on the verge of withering? This is not true of me now. I only write what I consider absolutely essential.

* * * * *

Those facts, words, persons remembered are, in themselves, eternal facts. For that which is experienced is remembered and is possible only with a continual emphasizing of what is already familiar, experienced—as a formulated character of an event. I can recall what I saw but not recover how I felt. The poet is one who, by virtue of his nature, reacts in a special way to both memory and remembrance.

A circumstance may occur, which hinders my presence where I am expected. My presence could be useful there as well as where I find myself. I should not want to give freely of myself to just anyone: my days of trust, of cheerfulness, of profound moments that come of important relationships. I set the highest value on those of my own temperament, which is I suppose natural. Though I may have a casual experience with someone, when I come to an intimate affair I behave according to immensely various and complex systems of association. I am even more austere about friendship than I am about love. It's been said I find friendships less rewarding. Not so. I value my friends all the more because they are not a trap for my love.

* * * * *

. . . looking at someone carries the implicit expectation that our look will be returned by the object of our gaze. Where this expectation is met (which, in the case of thought processes, can apply equally to the look of the eye of the mind and to a glance pure and simple), there is an experience of the aura to the fullest extent. . . . The person we look at, or who feels she is being looked at, looks at us in turn.

—Walter Benjamin, *Illuminations*

Who can say what a poem will stimulate, excite, provoke? I do not write from any desire for self-advancement, or to exercise a talent, or derive a fortune from it. I *must* write, always, "out of deep need" [Louis Zukofsky]—the need to express what force and meaning are in me. Poetry is a calling; it cannot be chosen, and those who are chosen by it have no choice but to obey.

> *Art is a curious command*
> *We must do what we are bidden*
> *to do and can go only so far*
> *as the light permits.*
>
> —William Carlos Williams

To be a poet is a commitment. Wordsworth saw the poet's as a "priest-like task". I came upon my task almost accidentally. But once the issue was joined, my work proved to be intimately related to impulse and to the stubbornness of my one-way will. I had to test whether the established world would crush me, or whether I could dislodge a piece of the world's outworn fundaments and make a place for a new one.

*   *   *   *   *

I am the opposite of the virtuous man; but I recognize virtue just because it does not desire to be recognized. I make of myself what I can: partly what I *must*, partly what gives me pleasure, or seems beneficial to me in some way. What I have created has branded me a seducer. But if I follow my inclinations, or the demands of necessity or usefulness, then I should neither praise nor blame myself nor let others praise or blame me.

Presently, I am back at my flat above the rumble of East 14th Street—as good a place as any to work in and easy to maintain. There are days when much is accomplished. I can go away when and where I please for as long as I please. I can set sail at any hour, a stranger to despair. I realize how difficult a sketch of myself can become, which is not an apology for a life but a research into its nature, as I deal with my relation to the person to whom the original notes for this piece were addressed. In the early course of it, I wrote myself out of a mood of discontent, and reassured myself about love

157

during that phase of boredom, restlessness and vexation. This autobiographical experiment has achieved its purpose in the attempt to satisfy my curiosity about life and the world. If I did not take an immense interest in life, through the medium of myself—in the form of photography and poetry—I should not have embarked upon this self-scrutiny. Curiosity transforms.

*   *   *   *   *

A vaillans coeurs, riens impossible

—Jacques Coeur

I have perhaps explained too much. I could have been out sailing or riding, or doing a work-out at the gym. I have not lost the ability to laugh, if laughter may be allowed in serious matters. I could harm myself by letting people know me entirely, or even one person know me well. Of whom am I speaking? We have become and are still strangers to each other. We are too different to resume in any enduring fashion, though this is no reason for eschewing reconciliation. But should we meet ten years hence—the matter of time is indisputable to the reality itself—, I'd wager that we would be mistaken in one another again. The encounter would not be the tender and loyal embrace of understanding, not attraction, but the repulsion of misunderstanding. She could never admit having sublimated herself to my sexual desire.

She fears honesty, fears losing fortunes, fears living and dying, and fears others. She denies and tends to abolish the Other. Thus, we emerge as one another's Nemesis. Still, Time is always offering occasions that disclose their value. The unlikely situation might suddenly present itself: a fine winter's day, shot through with high-contrasts. The pavement red, orange and black. 5 p.m.—"the golden hour," like they say. We would meet again in a mood of limitless friendship, free from the sting of past fixation. The encounter would become tranquil from trusting that all things could turn out well. How honest and confidential we could be, telling seemingly all that rests in the mind, and yet go away feeling what we had in mind to say was yet unsaid, because what often overwhelms is the memory that what had been strived for may have been nearer, truer, and its attachment infinitely tender, at some other time, and also because of the incapacity to know each other as lovers again, or even in some new way. Williams has said it similarly in two poems:

> I shall pass her on the street
> We shall say trivial things
> to each other . . .
>
> > [from "The Revelation"]

*

> In New York, it is said,
> they do meet (if that is
> what is wanted) talk but
> nothing is exchanged . . .
>
> > [from "A Place (Any Place)
> > to Transcend All Places"]

This hypothetical tale. . . Life often appears to imitate art and as Alberto Moravia points out:

> Art is not like life, life is like art, but it cannot know this unless Art, in all its successive and varied forms, its continual assertion of itself in the midst of meaninglessness, shows life that this is so and thereby teaches it how to be.

I am not foolish enough to think that all suspicions would vanish upon re-encounter or that she realize all that I said, did, and wanted, was right. Lost opportunities. Who cares. . .? Speculation of such a meeting is an expression of both my fears and wishes, and yet I am powerless to bring that day nearer. Trust cannot be predicted and nowhere is it pure. One can only have misgivings where one has before had trust. Such separations, being what they are, allow the formation of new relationships, more friendly to the growth of character. They permit the reception of new influences that will be of profound worth in the next years.

* * * * *

Buddha never wrote a line. Socrates was an enemy of writing. Jesus spoke his sermon. Lao-Tse limited himself to 83 phrases. The Maha Prajna Hridaya Pāramitā Sūtra uses less than 300 words to answer the entire riddle of the universe. Its meaning is whatever one may choose to call meaning. [*That which exists through itself is what is called meaning.* —Charles Olson.]

* * * * *

I am suddenly aware as I write this that I've learned something I needed to know before I began: One does not get over a love by representing it; rather, it is over when one becomes able to represent it.

I have been described as having the stubborn persistency of one whose gaze cannot be deflected from the actual fact before me: what I see, I write. Yet I believe the mind distinguishes between impressions and does not have to agree with what the eyes see. One does not grow tired of beauty, but does grow tired of what is pleasing, of what only flatters the senses. In this instance, then, love needs a more intrinsic reality than a bodily appearance—how terrible to discover one has been loving an illusion.

Her intelligence invents her beauty and is what I desire. The more intelligent the more beautiful a person becomes. A parallel statement is Kierkegaard's: "Temptation tends to make a person more beautiful." The essence of intelligence—which is inexplicable—is dearer than mere beauty and gives a higher pleasure ultimately.

Hanns Sachs, a pupil of Freud, suggested that beauty caused sadness. He observed that "pure beauty drives those who are willing and able enough for its reception back into the depths of their inner self. . . . It supersedes all their other interests and makes them feel sad. The badge of true beauty is sadness."

160

According to Dr. Sachs, the perception of what he calls pure beauty is an intense and isolating experience. "The difficulty," he concludes, "is not how to understand beauty, but how to be able to stand it." In like instance, Rilke writes ["First Elegy"]:

> *Because beauty's nothing*
> *but the start of terror we can hardly bear,*
> *and we adore it because of the serious scorn*
> *it would kill us with.*

> (trans. A. Poulin, Jr.)

In his essay on Baudelaire, T. S. Eliot said that "in much romantic poetry, the sadness is due to the exploitation of the fact that no human relations are adequate to human desires, but also the disbelief in any further object for human desires than that which, being human, fails to satisfy them."

It is I who create what I desire. I do not insist that beauty be unusual, or that it be so because I desire it—only that it be intelligent. Desire magnifies that which one desires; it grows even more by not being fulfilled. The greater my desire for a person grows, the more value I ascribe to that person. And my own desire is of supreme value to me. For some people love is a violent desire [Phaedra], for others a work of art [Beatrice]. Camus has said, "Everything that stands in the way of desire—principally society—must therefore be mercilessly destroyed."

*   *   *   *   *

Nothing is inevitable until after it happens. In this world, change is the only constant—an inward change in the individual: its presence is all we can affirm, coming at every moment and at every moment not yet arrived. The character of life is that which remains the same throughout. *Plus ça change, plus c'est la même chose.* The cliché. The only permanence is change, which is in our nature, and is simply a matter of experience. Nothing is secure but change. It belongs to the essence. It is everywhere, it is nowhere. You go to a museum to look at a Giotto and you end up discovering, or being discovered by, a stranger. Chance of eyes even, passing glance. Everything and nothing is left to chance.

*　*　*　*　*

It is not vanity when I say my strength lies in self-consciousness. Consciousness is present only to the extent that it is useful—as a tool and particular aspect of the total life. Consciousness—the recognition of oneself—increases in value in proportion as it increases in clarity. Consciousness is the noblest human quality: that I say 'I' or can will *something*. In my self I can see possibilities; I can imagine all things as being other than what they are. I fulfill myself by choosing what is painful and difficult and necessary. I knowingly collect from everything and everyone I see, hear, live through, my *sum*. I am then a principle of selection—I am the opposite of a heroic nature—, I discard much. I take risks. I run ahead of myself: I foresee my own death.

14:vi:82

The Winery,
Chestnut Ridge,
Millbrook, New York

Printed May 1983 in Santa Barbara & Ann Arbor for the
Black Sparrow Press by Graham Mackintosh & Edwards
Brothers Inc. Design by Barbara Martin. This edition is
published in paper wrappers; there are 200 hardcover
copies numbered & signed by the author; & 26 lettered
copies handbound in boards by Earle Gray each with a
page of original manuscript by the author.   99

Gerard Malanga was associated with Andy Warhol from 1963 to 1970 as silk-screen technician, photo-researcher, cinematographer and superstar. In 1969 they co-founded / co-edited *Interview* and it was during this time that Malanga began taking pictures as a direct outgrowth from his own film-making. In 1972 he studied Tibetan Law and Philosophy with lama Geshey Ngawang Dargay in northern India. He has edited numerous publications and literary projects, including *Little Caesar #9 / "Unprecedented Information"* (1979), *Angus MacLise Checklist 1959-1979* (1981, Dia Art Fdn) and *Photovoyeurism*, a survey with thirty-four photographers. Besides his own photographic work, Malanga has written *UP-TIGHT!: The Velvet Underground Story* with Victor Bockris and is presently compiling a book of poems and pictures, entitled *Three Diamonds*. He divides his time between New York City and the Massachusetts Berkshires. He has previously published four books with Black Sparrow Press, *The Last Benedetta Poems* (1969), *10 Poems for 10 Poets* (1970), *Incarnations: Poems 1965-1971* (1974) and *Ten Years After: The Selected Benedetta Poems* (1977).

Photo: John Hersey